THE HISTORY OF THE NEW ORLEANS SAINTS

Published by Creative Education
123 South Broad Street
Mankato, Minnesota 56001
Creative Education is an imprint of The Creative Company.

DESIGN AND PRODUCTION BY **EVANSDAY DESIGN**

LIBRARY OF CONGRESS CATALOGING-IN-PUBLICATION DATA

Bell, Lonnie.
The history of the New Orleans Saints / by Lonnie Bell.
p. cm. — (NFL today)
Summary: Highlights the key personalities and memorable games in
the history of the seaport city's popular football team.
ISBN 1-58341-305-7
1. New Orleans Saints (Football team)—History—Juvenile
literature. [1. New Orleans Saints (Football team)—History.
2. Football—History.] I. Title. II. Series.

GV956.N366B45 2004
796.332'64'0976335—dc22   2003063099

First edition

9 8 7 6 5 4 3 2 1

COVER PHOTO: running back Deuce McAllister

PHOTOGRAPHS BY
AP/Wide World Photos, Corbis (Bettmann, Reuters, UPI/Corbis-Bettmann, Troy Wayrynen/Columbian/NewSport),
Getty Images, Icon Sports Media Inc., SportsChrome USA

NEW ORLEANS, LOUISIANA, WAS FOUNDED IN 1718 ON A SWAMPY BEND IN THE MISSISSIPPI RIVER ABOUT 50 MILES NORTH OF THE GULF OF MEXICO. AT THE TIME, FEW COULD HAVE IMAGINED HOW GRAND THE CITY WOULD BECOME. IN 1803, FRANCE SOLD THE LOUISIANA TERRITORY TO THE UNITED STATES FOR $15 MILLION. IT WAS QUITE A BARGAIN; THE SALE INCLUDED 827,000 SQUARE MILES—AND THE CITY NICKNAMED "THE BIG EASY."

SINCE THAT TIME, NEW ORLEANS HAS BECOME FAMOUS FOR ITS ANNUAL MARDI GRAS FESTIVAL AND ITS KEY ROLE IN THE DEVELOPMENT OF JAZZ MUSIC. IN 1967, THIS PARTY-LOVING CITY GAINED ADDITIONAL FAME AS THE BIRTHPLACE OF A NEW NATIONAL FOOTBALL LEAGUE (NFL) FRANCHISE. ONE OF THE MOST POPULAR JAZZ SONGS AMONG THE CITIZENS OF NEW ORLEANS WAS "WHEN THE SAINTS GO MARCHIN' IN." SO IT WAS ONLY FITTING THAT THE NEW TEAM, DECKED OUT IN UNIFORMS OF GOLD AND BLACK, WAS NAMED THE SAINTS.

[1967 New Orleans Saints]

THE SAINTS MARCH IN>

LIKE MOST NEW teams, the first-year Saints were a mixture of aging players and inexperienced rookies. Tom Fears, a former NFL receiver, was hired as the team's first head coach. Coach Fears was so tough and demanding that players complained his practices were "like a three-hour ride in a washing machine." New Orleans ended its first season 3–11, tying the NFL record for wins by an expansion team.

Among the Saints' best players in their early years were quarterback Billy Kilmer, cornerback Dave Whitsell, and wide receiver Danny Abramowicz. Of these, Abramowicz contributed perhaps the most. In 1969, the young receiver—who had not been selected until the 17th round of the NFL Draft in 1967—caught 73 passes for more than 1,000 yards.

Danny Abramowicz led all New Orleans receivers in catches in the franchise's first five seasons.

In 1969, the Saints added another key player: talented placekicker Tom Dempsey. Dempsey had been born without a right hand and with no toes on his right foot, but that didn't stop him from earning a special place in the NFL record books. In one game in 1970, New Orleans trailed the Detroit Lions 17–16 with just seconds remaining. At the time, the longest field goal in NFL history was a 56-yarder. Dempsey lined up a 63-yard attempt and booted the ball through the goal posts, setting a long-distance record that would go unmatched for 18 years. Even though the Saints posted their fourth losing record that season, fans hoped that Dempsey's kick was a sign of good things to come.

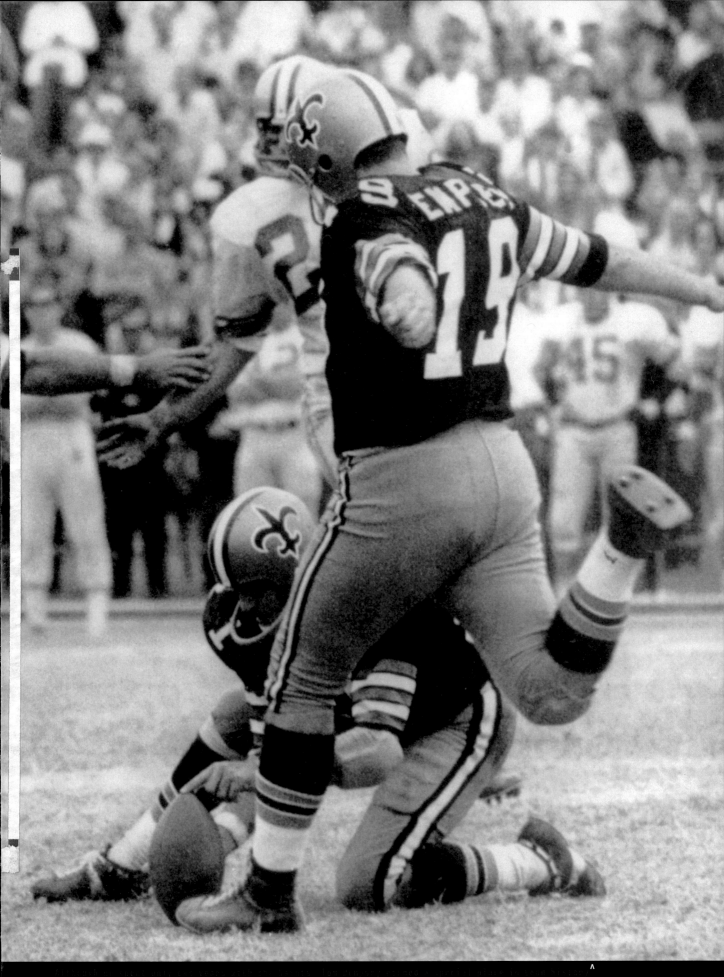

THE ARCHIE MANNING YEARS>

IN 1971, NEW ORLEANS fans found another reason for

optimism: a rookie quarterback named Archie Manning.

In Manning's first game, the Saints faced the Los Angeles

Rams, a team New Orleans had never beaten. Although

constantly hounded by a fierce Rams defense, Manning

passed for one touchdown, and ran for another on the

final play of the game to seal a 24–20 Saints victory.

That was just the beginning of a terrific career. Over the

course of 11 seasons in New Orleans, the scrappy quar-

terback would appear in two Pro Bowls and set virtually

every team passing record.

New Orleans tried to build a champion in the early 1970s

by bringing in such talented players as safety Tommy

Myers. But the team never really jelled. As the Saints

suffered one losing season after another, they became

Playing behind a shaky offensive line, quarterback Archie Manning often had to scramble for yards.

Down! Touch ❚❚ Set! Hut Hut!

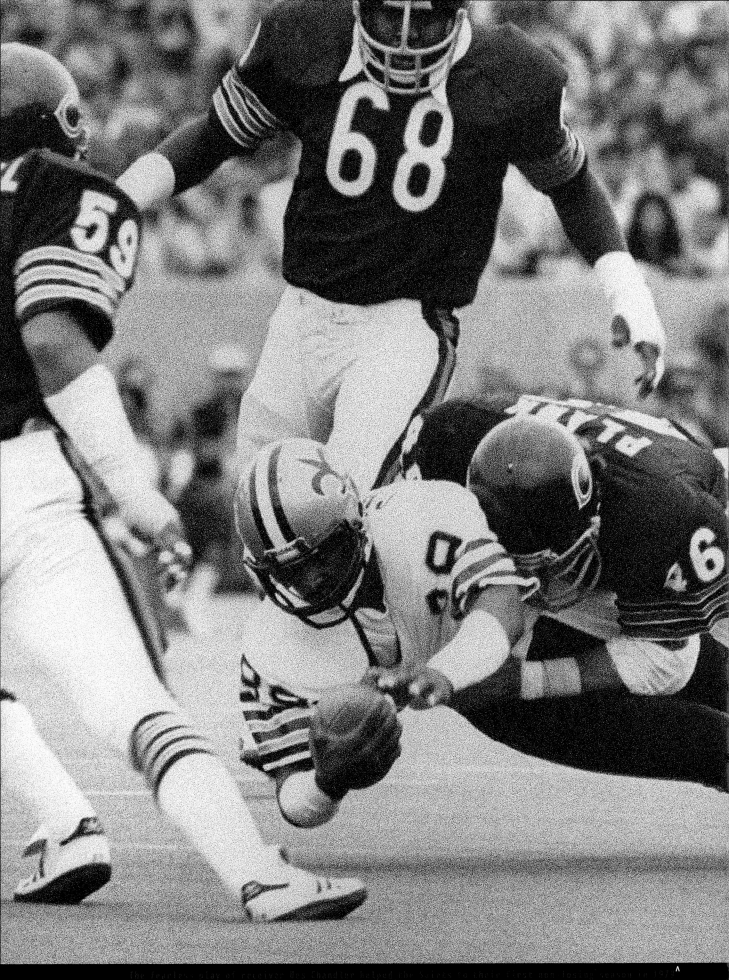

known as a one-man team—the one man being Manning. "I've always said Archie was a franchise player without a franchise," Hank Stram, who became the Saints' head coach in 1976, later said. "He'd be in the Hall of Fame if he'd had better players around him."

In the late '70s, Coach Stram attempted to do two things: surround Manning with better talent, and fill the nearly 70,000 seats in the new Louisiana Superdome. The Saints took a step in the right direction by selecting running backs Chuck Muncie and Tony Galbreath in the 1976 NFL Draft, but they remained at the bottom of the National Football Conference (NFC) Western Division standings in 1976 and 1977. Things finally began looking sunnier in New Orleans in 1978. That year, Manning threw for 3,416 yards and was named the NFC Player of the Year as the Saints went 7–9.

In 1979, the team jumped to 8–8. Muncie ran wild that season for a team-record 1,198 yards, speedy young receiver Wes Chandler set another club record with 1,069 receiving yards, and Myers headed an improved defense. It appeared that Manning at last had the supporting cast he needed to make the Saints contenders. "We're going to be there very soon," linebacker Joe Federspiel told reporters. "This town is dying for a winner, and everyone on this team is dying to be one."

SADLY, "DYING" IS just what the Saints did in 1980. The club lost its first 14 games, and most of the scores weren't even close. The defense collapsed completely, and the offense sputtered after Muncie was traded away. By midseason, newspapers began referring to the team as the "Ain'ts."

The hopes of Saints fans were rekindled in 1981, when former Houston Oilers coach O.A. "Bum" Phillips was named head coach. Phillips was a colorful character who paced the sidelines in blue jeans, cowboy boots, a western shirt, and a Stetson hat. In Houston, Coach Phillips had built a powerful team around star running back Earl Campbell. He set out to build the same type of team in New Orleans around rookie running back George Rogers.

Known for his unique fashion style, coach Bum Phillips spent five seasons on the Saints sidelines.

Early '80s star George Rogers had the speed to go around defenders or the power to go through them.

Rogers had won the 1980 Heisman Trophy as the best college player in the country while at the University of South Carolina, and he wasted no time in becoming an NFL star. In his first year (1981), he led the league in rushing with a jaw-dropping 1,674 yards and easily earned NFL Rookie of the Year honors.

But Rogers wasn't the only gem the Saints plucked from the 1981 NFL Draft. The team also drafted line-backer Rickey Jackson and tight end Hoby Brenner, both of whom would wear New Orleans black and gold for 13 seasons. During those years, Jackson would set club records for quarterback sacks (123) and games played (195), and Brenner would become a fine blocker and receiver.

By 1982, Manning was beginning to slow down, so Phillips convinced Oilers quarterback Ken Stabler to join the Saints. Two years later, Phillips also brought Earl Campbell to New Orleans. Campbell was nearing the end of his amazing NFL career, but Phillips believed the Hall-of-Famer still had something left in his powerful legs. "Earl Campbell may not be in a class by himself," Phillips said, "but whatever class he's in, it doesn't take long to call the roll."

With this new talent, the Saints came within seconds of nailing down their first winning season and a playoff berth in 1983. But in the final game of the year, the Los Angeles Rams kicked a last-second field goal to hand the Saints a 26–24 loss and leave them with an 8–8 mark. After the team fell to 5–11 in 1985, Phillips left town and Campbell retired. Rogers was traded away a year later. Saints fans began to wonder if things would ever change.

A quick and aggressive pass rusher, linebacker Rickey Jackson netted 12 sacks in both 1983 and 1984.

WINNERS AT LAST>

WHEN NEW ORLEANS businessman Tom Benson bought

the Saints in 1985, he made his expectations clear. "There is

a difference between wanting to win and having to win," he

said. "In our case, we have to win. We have to put in extra ef-

fort that leads to achievement. When you have to win, you

really look for the extra things that can make you successful."

One of those "extra things" was head coach Jim Mora, who

took over in 1986. Mora fined, benched, and cut players un-

til he found the right combination. Running back Rueben

Mayes burst onto the scene with 1,353 rushing yards that

year; Rickey Jackson, Pat Swilling, and Sam Mills formed per-

haps the NFL's top linebacker trio; and Morten Andersen—a

soccer player from Denmark—proved to be an accurate, long-

range kicker. Behind these players, New Orleans went 7–9.

The 1987 season was the Saints' 21st. Before the season

began, Benson issued a challenge to his players by telling

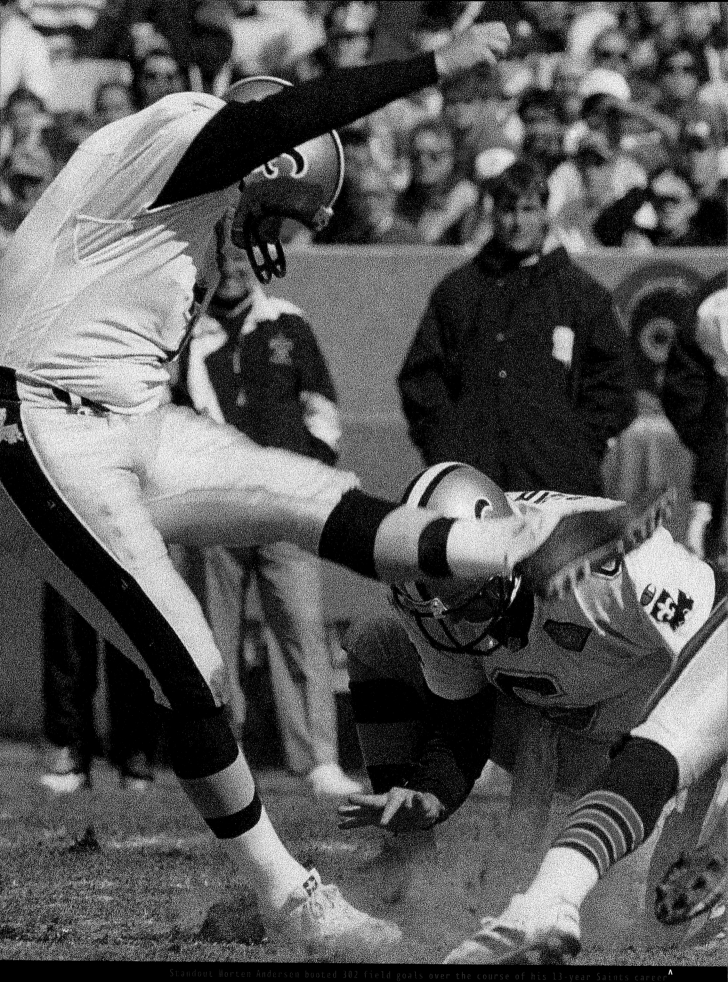

Standout Morten Andersen booted 302 field goals over the course of his 13-year Saints career.

reporters, "When you're 21, you become a man." The Saints seemed to get the message, winning their last nine games of the year en route to a 12–3 finish—their first winning season. To no one's surprise, Mora was named NFL Coach of the Year.

In their first-ever playoff game, the Saints faced the Minnesota Vikings in front of 68,000 wild fans in the Superdome. After the opening kickoff, New Orleans marched down the field and scored to take a 7–0 lead. But fans had little to cheer about after that as the Vikings went on to win in a 44–10 rout.

The Saints remained near the top of the NFC standings in the seasons that followed, making the playoffs again in 1990, 1991, and 1992. Unfortunately, they fell in the first round of the playoffs every time. "We've come a long way since that first season," said Coach Mora. "But it's not important where we've been. It's where we're going. We want to be the best team in the NFL."

Sadly, just as the Saints seemed ready to reach the Super Bowl, they began to slide back down the standings. After going 12–4 in 1992, the Saints fell from the playoff picture the next three years. "I think there will be a lot of soul-searching done by everyone on the team," offensive tackle Richard Cooper said of the Saints' decline. "These have been the kinds of seasons you wake up thinking about...for a long time."

Known for his great open-field moves, speedster Rueben Mayes treated fans to some superb performances.

IN 1994, QUARTERBACK Jim Everett arrived in New Orleans to help turn things around. During eight years with the Los Angeles Rams, Everett had passed for more than 3,000 yards in five straight seasons—one of the most impressive streaks in the NFL. Coach Mora was excited about the addition. "In my opinion, Everett is one of the top quarterbacks in the league," Mora said. "He's got stats that are right up there with the best."

In 1995, Everett proved his coach right by passing for 3,970 yards and 26 touchdowns—both new club records. But when the Saints dropped to 3–13 the next year, the team's shakeup continued. Mora quit midway through the season and was soon replaced by former Chicago Bears coach "Iron" Mike Ditka.

A tall passer with a strong arm, Jim Everett did his best to change the Saints' fortunes in the mid-1990s.

In the best season of his short New Orleans career (2001), Ricky Williams charged for 1,245 yards ^

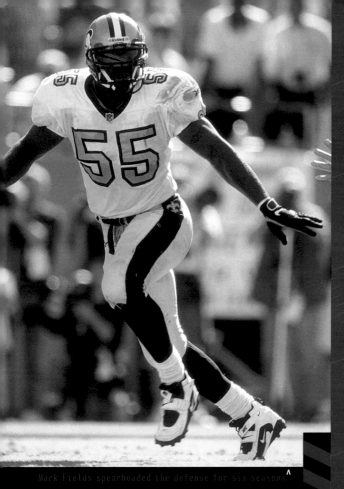
Mark Fields spearheaded the defense for six seasons ^

Quarterback Aaron Brooks was an elusive scrambler ^

The Saints posted 6–10 records in their first two seasons under Coach Ditka. The team's defense—featuring hard-hitting linebacker Mark Fields and safety Sammy Knight—had become one of the NFL's best, but Everett had left town, and the offense was weak. So, in 1999, Coach Ditka made a bold move, trading eight draft picks to the Washington Redskins for the right to select University of Texas running back Ricky Williams in the NFL Draft.

Williams had been a college star, rushing for 2,124 yards and winning the Heisman Trophy during his senior season in 1998. Unfortunately, he would never become the savior the Saints needed. Williams struggled with injuries and personal problems in New Orleans, and he would be traded away after only three seasons. After the Saints went just 3–13 in 1999, Ditka was fired and replaced by former Pittsburgh Steelers defensive coordinator Jim Haslett.

Coach Haslett found a winning combination in New Orleans, and much quicker than anyone expected. The key to the turnaround was young quarterback Aaron Brooks, who emerged as a star after being named a starter late in the 2000 season. Playing behind outstanding offensive tackle William Roaf, the fleet-footed quarterback led the Saints to a 10–6 finish and their first-ever playoff victory—a 31–28 win over the St. Louis Rams.

Although the Saints narrowly missed the play-offs in 2001, 2002, and 2003, there was plenty of optimism in New Orleans. With Brooks, speedy receiver Joe Horn, and defensive linemen Darren Howard and Charles Grant, the Saints boasted a solid lineup on both sides of the ball. New Orleans had also found its long-awaited star running back in Deuce McAllister. The 6-foot-1 and 230-pound McAllister—who ran like a deer and hit like a truck—delighted fans by charging for more than 1,300 yards in both 2002 and 2003. "Deuce knows we're counting on him," said Brooks, "and it's his time to shine."

Although it took the New Orleans Saints 21 years to record their first winning season, their fans have always stayed patient and loyal. Over the years, those fans have watched their Saints march into the playoffs five times and enjoyed the heroics of such stars as Archie Manning, Rickey Jackson, and Deuce McAllister. When the Saints do finally bring home a Super Bowl trophy, there will undoubtedly be a big party in New Orleans, a city that really knows how to celebrate.

INDEX >